LOVE & FREE

爱·自由

Bo Zhang / 张博 著

Dedication

This book is dedicated to Mr. Ayumu Takahashi (高橋歩) for the beautiful and powerful messages conveyed through his publications, which have profoundly inspired my life. To my beloved parents, my friend Sumi Wei, and to all those whom I love and have loved — you infuse great meaning into my life within this unique world of mine.

CONTENTS · 目录

等待
The Wait

平行世界
Parallel Worlds

天秤座 vs. 处女座
Libra vs. Virgo

暗恋
Secret Crush

触电的感觉
Ecstatic Schock

心动
Crush on You

妳
YOU

愿望清单
Wishlist

爱称
The Nicknames I Calll You

我与世界
Me & The World

旅行
Travel

CONTENTS · 目录

你的香味
Your Fragrance

恋爱的季节
Season of Love

爱
Love

我爱你
I Love You

彼岸
The Other Shore

自由
Free

我不怕一觉不醒
I'm Not Afraid of Not Waking Up

美好的人
Beautiful Souls

田园 · 都市
Pastoral · Urban

21
Twenty-one

CONTENTS · 目录

朋友？笔友？
Friends? Pen-pals?

我
Me

自由
Free

自由
Free

爱·自由
Love · Free

等待

等待花开的过程是美好的
就像我等待飞机落地见到你的那一刻

The Wait

The entire process of watching flowers to bloom is beautiful,
Just like the moment I was waiting for the plane to land and see you.

平行世界

我
一边和你在这世界里
分享着世俗的一切
早晨起床后的问候
你路过的建筑
因为上班迟到　你在雨中的奔跑
和今天你喜欢的食物

这让我觉得温暖

与这个时空平行的
是我的另一个世界
——我小心翼翼地守护的秘密空间
这空间是我带着滤镜的一扇窗
是我神秘的翅膀
这让我觉得特别
特别的你
特别的我
和特别的我们

在这空间里
一切都和你距离遥远
一切又都和你有关
我听着喜欢的音乐
呼吸着甜味的空气
和陌生人擦肩
和我的想象遇见
和更好的自己并肩

我的翅膀带着我和你
穿越时空的界限
在这空间里自由地飞翔

这空间
让我对另一个平行世界的你
和你的笑脸
莫名想念

这空间奇妙神奇
定格和你有关的所有美好瞬间
想你的时候
一秒钟的穿越
你就出现在眼前

我在这两个平行世界不断地切换
此刻我比刚才又多爱你一点

Parallel Worlds

In one world
I'm sharing the mundane aspects with you,
Greetings in the morning after waking up,
The buildings you pass by,
Your hurried run in the rain because you're late for work,
And the food you enjoy today.

It makes me feel real and warm.

Parallel to this time and space,
Exists my other world,
A secret space I carefully guard.
This space is a window with my filter,
My mysterious wings,
It makes me feel special,
The special you,
The special me,
And the special us.

In this space,
Everything is distant from you,
Yet everything is related to you.
I listen to my favorite music,
Breathe in the light air,
Brush shoulders with strangers,
And encounter my imagination.
A better version of myself stands side by side.

My wings take me with you,
Crossing the boundaries of time and space,
Freely soaring in this space.

This space
Makes me miss the you in another parallel world,
And your smiling face, inexplicably.

This space is magical and wonderful,
Freezing all the beautiful moments related to you.
When I miss you,
A second's journey,
And you appear before my eyes.

I constantly switch between these two parallel worlds,
Right now, I love you more than just a moment ago.

天秤座 vs. 处女座

这种感觉
似曾相识

似有似无
捉摸不定
想紧紧抓住
又胆怯到想要把她推远

这感觉
熟悉又陌生
使我紧张
又让我无力

紧张到
想到她的名字
就心跳加速呼吸局促
无力到
好想逃到地球之外的太空

当我开始因为她
早晨早醒
晚上辗转反侧
想念关于她的一切

这感觉
使我害怕 又让我"胆大"

害怕
这一切是真的
害怕
全部都是幻觉

胆大到
一秒钟就冲昏头脑
抓住她的手不顾一切
向整个世界宣告她的存在
胆大到
下一刻
可以和她划清界限
转身抛下她在身后茫茫的人海

这感觉
它是爱情么

也许
让我害怕的
是愈合的心脏重新跳动
是那个沉睡的自己开始苏醒
和死掉的爱情再次复活

也许
这感觉
该停止在
这想爱未爱 将见未见的一刻
这一刻的世界
这一刻的她
和这一刻的我们

Libra vs. Virgo

This feeling
feels familiar

Faint yet palpable
Elusive and uncertain
Wanting to hold on tightly
Yet timidly wanting to push her away

This feeling
Familiar yet unfamiliar
Makes me nervous
Yet leaves me powerless

Nervous to the point
That thinking of her name
Accelerates my heartbeat and stops my breath
Powerless to the extent
That I wish to escape to the space beyond Earth

When I start waking up early because of you
Tossing and turning at night
Longing for everything about you

This feeling
Frightens me and emboldens me

Frightened
That all of this is real
Afraid
That it's all an illusion

Bold to the point
Of being intoxicated in a second
Grabbing your hand without a second thought
Announcing your existence to the entire world
Bold to the extent
That the next moment
I can draw a clear boundary with you
Turn around and leave you in the vast sea of people

Perhaps
What scares me
Is the mending heart starting to beat again
Is the dormant self beginning to awaken
And the love that seemed dead coming back to life

Perhaps
This feeling
Should stop at
This moment of wanting to love, of almost meeting
This moment's world
This moment's you
And this moment's us

暗恋

内心甜蜜的煎熬
和夜不能寐的辗转反侧
在白天和夜晚
将我拉近又推远

你的呼吸像轻柔的羽毛
你的讯息变成我心情的晴雨表

想知道你起床的样子
想听到你睡觉前的声音

多么想靠近你
默默守护着你

这是住在我身上的
另一个你的世界啊
你可以自由放松地做自己

我想骄傲放肆地喊你的名字

这种感觉
在我的内心消散了很久
今天你让我重新经历一遍！
I know I found comfort in my misery.

Secret Crush

Sweet torment within the heart,
And restless tossing and turning through the sleepless night,
In both day and night,
It draws me close and then pushes me away.

Your breath is like gentle feathers,
Your messages become the barometer of my mood.

I want to know how you look when you wake up,
I want to hear your voice before you sleep.

How i long to be close to you,
Silently guarding over you.

This is the world of another you
That resides within me,
Where you can freely relax and be yourself.

I want to proudly and boldly shout your name.

This feeling,
Had long dissipated within my heart,
But today, you make me relive it!
I know I found comfort in my misery.

触电的感觉

那天早上
车流密集
我小心翼翼地
试着牵你的手穿过马路

碰到你指尖的那一瞬间
一股强大的电流
从你柔软的手指
传到了我的掌心
然后从心脏到头顶

这强烈的感觉
像是触电
让我有点眩晕
我们是被幸福冲昏头脑的恋人

你半低着头
脸上略过一丝羞怯
安静乖巧地顺着拎着你手的方向
和我一起走到对面的马路边
我没有回头直视你的眼睛

Ecstatic Shock

That morning,
With dense traffic,
I cautiously
Tried to hold your hand to cross the road.

The moment I touched your fingertips,
A powerful current
Passed from your slender fingers
To the palm of my hand,
And then from my heart to the top of my head.

This intense sensation
Feels like an electric shock,
Leaving me a bit dizzy.
We are lovers overwhelmed by happiness.

You lowered your head slightly,
A hint of shyness passing over your face.
Quietly and tenderly, you followed the direction of the hand
I was holding,
Walking with me to the other side of the road.
I was too nervous to look back and meet your eyes.

心动

那天傍晚
在透明玻璃围绕的麦当劳餐厅里
我们面对面坐着

那是我第一次带你游览我的城市
你好安静！

那晚人声嘈杂
钟鼓楼繁华热闹如旧
用餐前
你微微低了下头
然后轻轻地
将你的长发从脖颈右侧捋到左侧

那一瞬间
你温柔的气息
不经意间将我的心弦拨动
看到你移去头发后肩膀露出的一角
我紧张到不敢跟你对视
于是悄悄低下了头

我那晚们撑着透明的雨伞
走在被雨淋湿的青色人行道上
我感觉你离我好近
又好像还很遥远

而我记忆深刻的画面
就是那一刻坐在我对面的你
和坐在鼓楼边西大街透明玻璃餐厅的我们

那天，你好美！

Crush on You

That evening,
In the McDonald's restaurant with transparent glass all around,
We sat facing each other.

It was my first time showing you around my city,
You were quiet.

The night was bustling,
The Bell and Drum Tower lively as ever.
Before the meal,
You slightly lowered your head,
Then gently,
Swept your long hair from the right side of your neck to the left.

In that moment,
Your gentleness, without your notice,
Made my heart beat faster.
Seeing a part of your shoulder revealed after moving your hair,
I was so nervous I couldn't meet your gaze,
So I quietly lowered my head.

That night, holding a transparent umbrella,
We walked on the rain-soaked blue sidewalk.
I felt you were so close to me,
Yet somehow still distant.

But the most memorable scene of that day
Is that moment when you sat across from me,
And us, sitting in the transparent glass restaurant on the West Avenue beside the Drum Tower.

That day, you looked so beautiful!

妳

有妳在心里
我和万物都开始有了神秘的联系
略过指间的轻风
擦肩而过的路人
头顶的飞鸟
大海的声音

我可以决定花开的季节
天亮的时间
时钟的快慢
每日的天气
和早餐的味道

这一切美妙的变化
都是妳神奇的魔法

YOU

With you in my heart,
A mysterious connection begins with everything around me.
The gentle breeze passing through my fingers,
Pedestrians passing by,
The birds flying overhead,
The sound of the sea.

I can decide the season of blossoms,
The time of daybreak,
The speed of the clock,
The daily weather,
And the taste of breakfast.

All these magical changes
Happen because of the special you.

愿望清单

我们
好像遇见的时间很短
短到仿佛就那短短几秒的一面
我们遇见的时间仿佛又很长
长到后来我所有的生活好似初见面那几秒延续的彷徨

你好啊
拨动我心弦的人
你还好吗
让我念念不忘的人

和你的相遇
让我有种如梦初醒的感觉
仿佛之前的人生我从未清醒
仿佛之后的所见皆是一个清醒的梦

我们的相遇
真实而又虚幻
短暂而猝不及防

来不及许愿
也来不及看清你的脸庞
我曾无数次幻想
与你有关的生活的模样
那里
我可以细数你可能会喜欢的件件桩桩

跟你一起放烟火
陪你一起逛街
带你一起看电影
和你一起去海边
一起坐长途火车看沿途的风景
一起在飞机上数天上洁白的云朵，欣赏下面陆地海洋的轮廓
一起写一本恋爱的日记
一起去超市购物 买从未见过的新奇物品
一起逃课翘班去约会
一起吵架后红着眼睛再和好
一起坐轮渡去小岛过周末
一起自驾游去主题乐园
一起早起看海边的灯塔和山上的红叶
一起去滑雪一起露营
一起去看NBA和棒球比赛
一起去皮划艇和攀岩
……

我想送你和你一样好看的花
带你吃各地的美食
养你喜欢的小动物
听你喜欢的演唱会
接你上下班
和你去春游
有你的每一天都仿佛我生命的某种仪式感

Wishlist

The time we spent together feels too short,
Short to the extent that it feels like just a few fleeting seconds.
The time we encountered each other also seems long,
Long enough that my life seems to echo the confusion of those first few seconds afterward.

I hope you are well.
You are the one who had my heart at hello.
How have you been?
You are always on my mind.

The encounter with you
Gave me a feeling of waking up from a dream,
As if I was never awake in my life before meeting you,
As if everything afterward is a vivid dream.

Our encounter
Is real yet elusive,
Brief and unexpected.

No time for wishes,
No time to clearly see your face.
I've fantasized countless times
About what a life related to you might look like.
There,
I can enumerate everything you might like:

Setting off fireworks,
Strolling through the streets,
Watching movies,
Going to the seaside,
Taking a long train ride to see the scenery,
Counting the fluffy clouds from the plane and admiring the contours of the land and sea below,
Writing a diary of love,
Shopping at the supermarket for exotic items,
Skipping classes for a date,
Arguing, then making up with red eyes,
Taking a ferry to an island for the weekend,
Road tripping to a theme park,
Waking up early to see the lighthouse by the seaside and the red leaves on the mountain,
Skiing together, camping,
Watching NBA and baseball games,
Kayaking and rock climbing
The list can continue…

I want to give you flowers as beautiful as you,
Take you to eat delicacies from all over the world,
Raise the pets you like,
Attend concerts you enjoy,
Pick you up to and from work,
Go on a spring outing with you.

Every day with you is a celebration of my life.

Rhode Island, United States

Rhode Island, United States

爱称

我该用怎样亲密的名字来称呼你呢
你有那么多美好的一面
哪一个昵称都不能完整表达我们之间的亲密
和你的特别

你的眼神清澈温柔
你的呼吸轻盈像雪花
你淡淡香香的气息似天使
你俏皮可爱的样子是叛逆的公主
你专注时像电影里的熟悉又神秘的桥段

你开心的时候 我的整个世界都被融化
你落泪时 我的心像破碎的玻璃散落一地

我喜欢你读书时的安静
和你工作时的热情

我在你不在时想你
也在你身旁想你

你那么特别 那么美好
我该用怎样亲密的名字来称呼你呢

The Nicknames I Call You

How should I address you with an intimate nickname?
There so many beautiful things on you,
No single nickname can fully express the intimacy between us
And your uniqueness.

Your gaze is clear and sweet,
Your breath is light like snowflakes,
Your faint, fragrant aura is angelic,
Your playful and adorable demeanor is that of a naughty princess,
Your focused moments are like familiar yet mysterious scenes from a movie.

When you're happy, my entire world melts,
When you shed tears, my heart shatters like broken glass scattered on the floor.

I love when you're reading quietly,
And when you're working with passion.

I think of you when you're not around,
And I miss you when you're nearby.

You're special, you are beautiful,
How should I address you with an intimate nickname?

我与世界

我与这个世界的关系
从小时候到成人后的现在
一直不断变化

世界很大
我想去那里走一走看一看

世界很美好
我想爱想玩想吃想睡想旅行想感受探索未知世界的奥秘

世界很吵
千万种声音在每一刻提醒我如何去生活和过上流行的价值下的生活

世界终于慢下来
我在自己的脚步声里追寻属于自己的美好

Me & The World

My relationship with the world
From childhood to the present as an adult
Has been constantly changing.

The world is vast,
I want to go there, walk around, and see.

The world is beautiful,
I want to love, play, eat, sleep, travel, and explore the mysteries of the unknown world.

The world is noisy,
Countless voices remind me at every moment how to live and lead a life that meet the standards of the current popularized values.

The world finally slows down in me,
I chase after my beauty of life following my own footsteps.

旅行

身体在旅行的时候
我的心也跟着一起在旅行

无论身在何处
需要的时候
我的心不必跟身体一起
它会自己去旅行

Travel

When my body is on a journey, my heart travels along with it.

No matter where my body resides, when needed, my heart doesn't have to go with the body; it travels on its own.

你的香味

你的特别
不止是你擦的香水味

是你讲话时的表情
你的笑声
你温柔的语气
你委屈时噘起的小嘴
你不经意间流露的亲密
你在我面前自然的松弛感
和你在件件小事上细微的心意

你的特别
你的香味
在我脑海
在我的梦里
我吹过的风里
我经过的春夏和秋冬里
我路过的陌生人的笑脸上
在我下一站火车的出站口

你让"女生"这个词独特美好
我喜欢你就是你

Your Fragrance

Your uniqueness
Is more than just the scent of the perfume on you.

It's your expressions when you speak,
Your laughter,
The gentleness in your tone,
The pout of your lips when you feel wronged,
The intimacy you unconsciously reveal,
The natural ease you have in front of me,
And your kindness and sweetness revealed in every little thing.

Your uniqueness,
Your fragrance,
Lies in my mind,
In my dreams,
In the breeze on my face,
In the springs, summers, autumns, and winters I've passed,
On the smiling faces of strangers I've walked past,
At the exit of the next train station I'm heading to.

You make the word "she" uniquely beautiful.
I like you just as you are.

恋爱的季节

冬天好适合恋爱
丝丝的冷意
节日的氛围
和关于冬天的童话故事
让我的感官和情感变得敏感而细腻

雪花跳着舞替我说情话
围巾包裹着温柔的情丝
一阵冷风心有灵犀地
将你送到我的怀里

你握着一杯热奶茶
我的手叠在你的手上
你突然脸红不说话

我们说笑的一瞬
你呼出的那一团薄薄的气息
在空气中结成雾气
像一团云朵把我带到了云端里

白天我们传简讯讲电话
谈论着节日如何准备给我们爱的人惊喜
傍晚怕冷的我们俩回家
在路灯下你挤我我挤你慢悠悠前进
分不清背后的脚印哪个是你哪个是我

Season of Love

Winter is a beautiful season to fall in love:
A subtle chill,
The festive atmosphere,
And fairy tales about winter,
Make my senses and emotions sensitive and delicate.

Snowflakes dance, whispering sweet words for me,
A scarf wraps around gentle threads of affection.
A gust of cold wind, as if with a tacit understanding,
Brings you into my embrace.

You hold a cup of hot milk tea,
My hands rest atop yours.
Suddenly, your face blushes, words left unspoken.

In the moment of our laughter,
The thin breath you exhale forms a mist in the air,
Like a cloud carrying me to the skies.

During the day, we exchange text messages and talk on the phone,
Discussing the surprises that we prepare for our loved ones during the holidays.
In the evening, fearing the cold, we make our way home,
Under the streetlights, we jostle each other, slowly advancing.
The footprints behind us blur, making it hard to distinguish which ones are yours and which ones are mine.

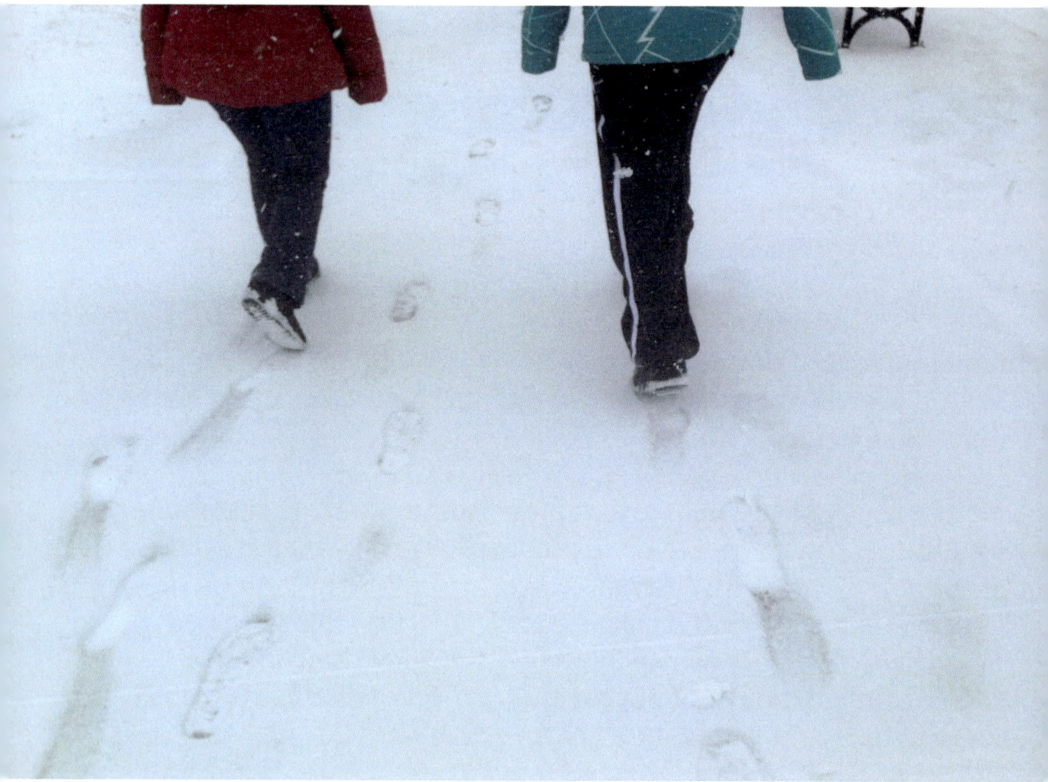

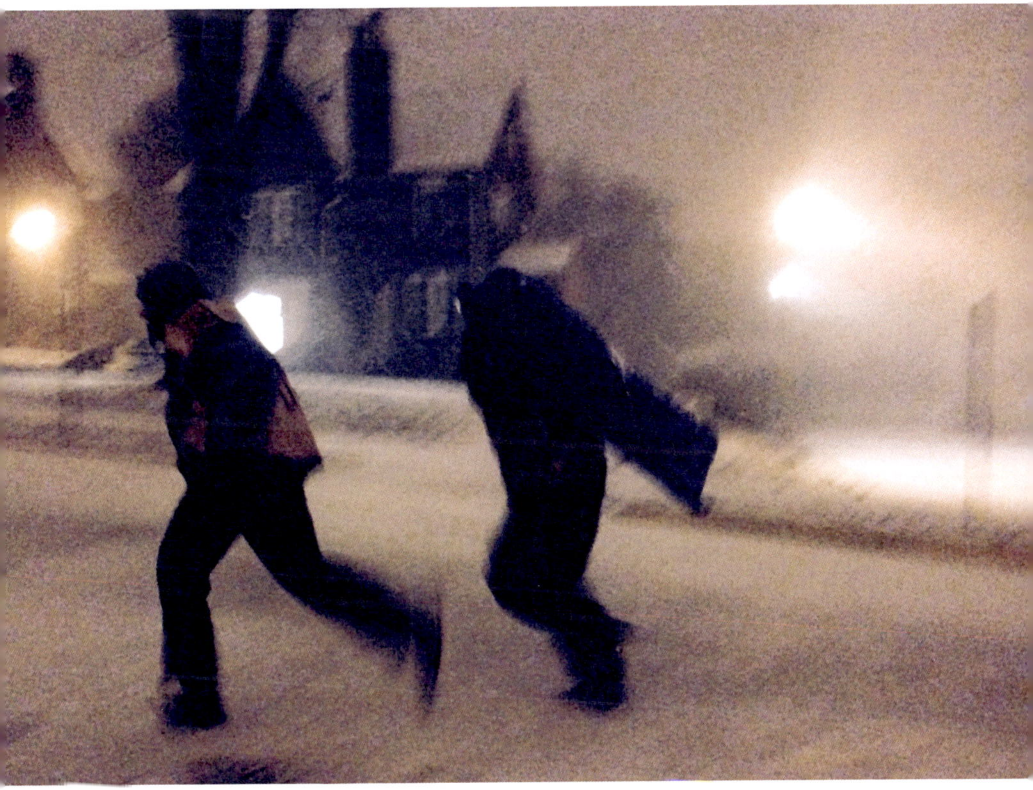

爱

爱是不安
是妒忌
是占有
是折磨人的坏东西

爱是安心
是成全
是付出
是让人神往的甜蜜

爱是
不能自拔
无法控制
不讲道理
毫无预兆
爱是天堂和地狱
爱是个矛盾体
好或者坏

可是
我却无法没有爱

Love

Love is uneasiness
It's jealousy,
It's the desire to possess,
It's the bitterness that tortures me.

Love is peace of mind,
It's fulfillment,
It's giving,
It's the sweet longing that captivates.

Love is irresistible,
Uncontrollable,
Unreasonable,
It happens without warning.
Love is both heaven and hell,
A contradiction of good and bad.

Nevertheless,
I cannot live without love.

我爱你

我爱你
而你永远是自由的

这让我总能反复喜欢上那个熟悉却不同的你

I Love You

I love you,
However, you are free.

This unrestrictedness allows me to repeatedly fall in love with the same yet different you.

彼岸

从孩童到成人
 没有到达的彼岸
一直是美好的：

将见未见的人恋人
寄出还未收到的一封信
即将认识的朋友
想要考入的大学
梦想旅行打卡的国家
即将确定关系的女朋友
飞机落地就见到的家人

这彼岸任我想象、驰骋、和主宰
这彼岸是我的王国
有任何我想要的样子
和我想要见和想要爱的人

但愿 我们终将到达梦想的彼岸
但愿 我们心里一直有彼岸

The Other Shore

From childhood to adulthood,
The unreached other shore is always beautiful:

Meeting the yet unseen lover,
Sending a letter yet to be received,
Hoping to befriend someone new,
Dreaming of entering a desired university,
Countries to be ticked off the travel bucket list,
The soon-to-be confirmed significant other,
Family waiting at the airport upon landing.

This other shore allows me to imagine, fantasize, and rule:
This other shore is my kingdom,
Taking any form I desire,
With the people I want to meet and love

... ...

May we eventually reach the shores of our dreams,
May there always be the other shore in our heart.

自由

做我喜欢做的事
吃我想吃的东西
去我想去的地方
见我想见的人
欣赏我想看的风景
这些让我感受到身体上的自由

而我心理上的自由
它可以是
写作
阅读
弹琴
绘画
做饭
想念
看海
听喜欢的音乐
爱自己喜欢的人
甚至
发呆
……

我原来如此自由

Free

Do what I love,
Eat what I crave,
Go where I desire,
Meet whom I long to see,
Appreciate the landscapes I yearn to behold.
These grant me a sense of physical freedom.

Yet, my mental freedom,
It can be reached through
Writing,
Reading,
Playing the piano,
Painting,
Cooking,
Yearning,
Watching the sea,
Listening to my favorite music,
Loving the people I cherish,
And even,
Daydreaming.
… …

I am, indeed, so free.

我不怕睡一觉不醒

我不怕一觉再也睡不醒

我只怕我眼里再也无光
再也看不到你
怕这世界少了一个爱你的人

I'm Not Afraid of Not Waking Up

I'm not afraid of never waking up from a sleep again.

I'm only afraid of the light fading from my eyes,
Of no longer being able to see you.

I fear a world with one less person who loves you.

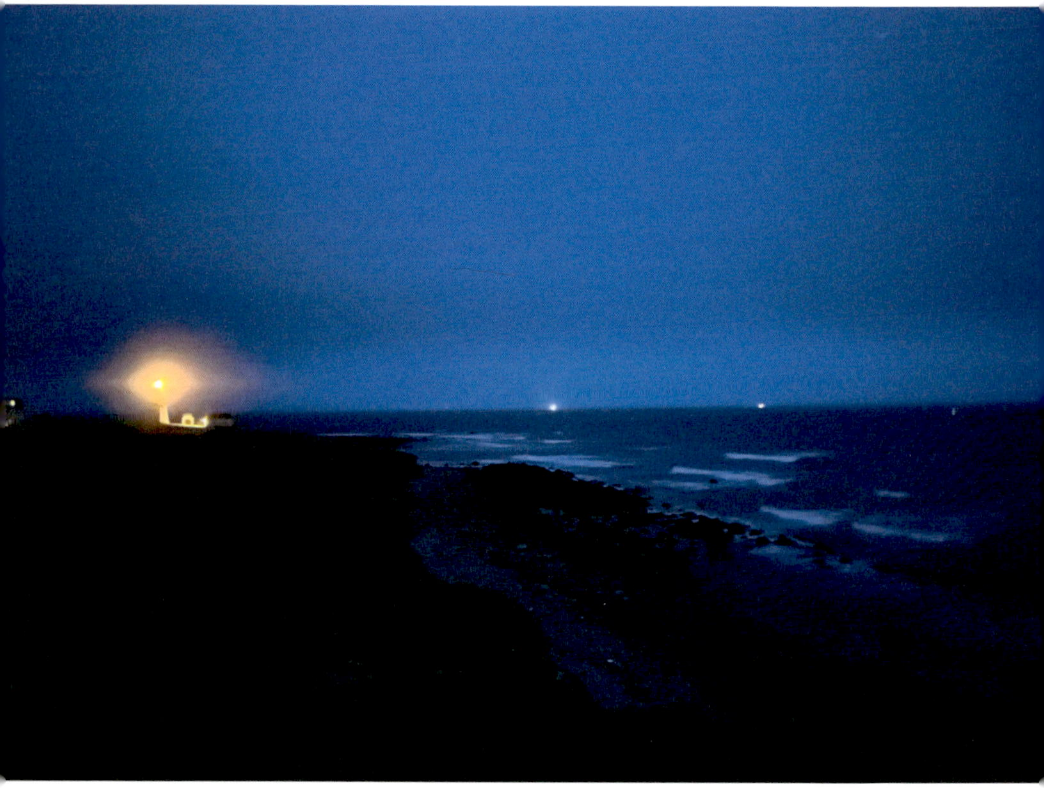

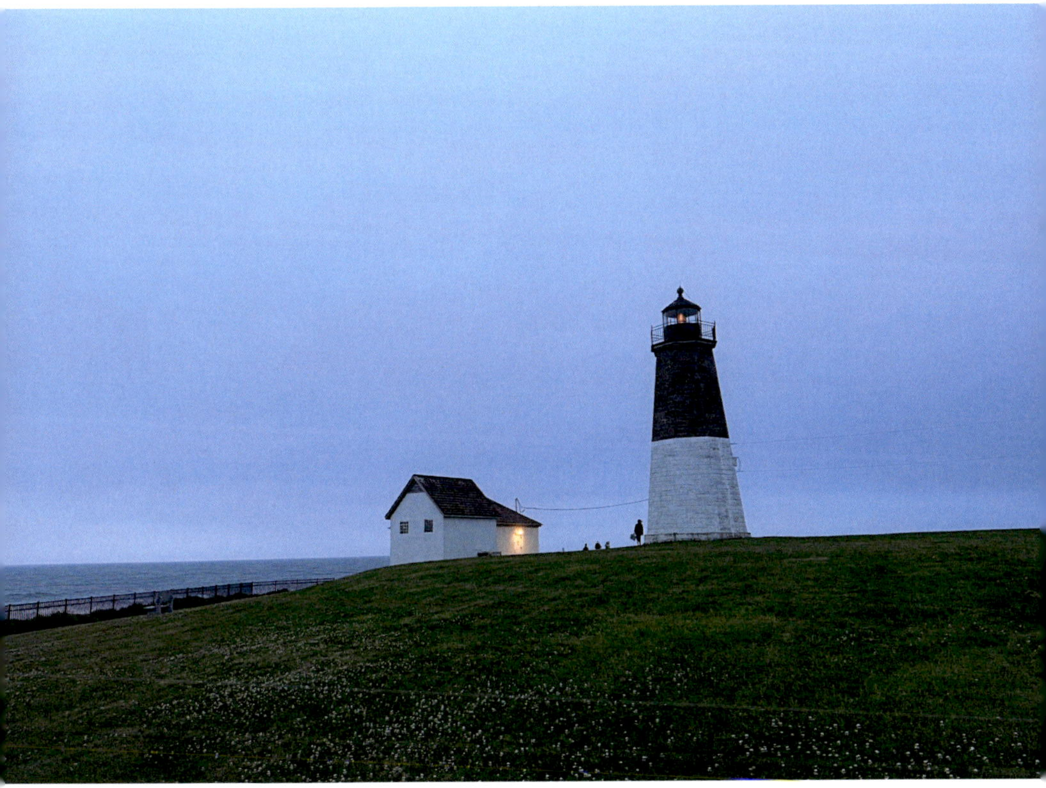

美好的人

生命中美好的人啊
自从遇见你,我的整个世界变成你的颜色
自从遇见你,我的整个世界是和你有关的形狀
这让我感到惊喜和满足

Beautiful Souls

The beautiful people in my life,
Since meeting you, my entire world has taken on your colors.
Since meeting you, my whole world is shaped by your presence.
This fills me with joy and contentment.

田园·都市

寄情于山水田园
我的心变得松弛而坚韧

融入到城市
我的心柔软而缤纷

我感恩自然的馈赠和人类文明的并存
让我对世界的感知丰富而有乐趣

Pastoral · Urban

Dwelling in the pastoral landscapes,
My heart becomes relaxed yet resilient.

Merging into the urban sprawl,
My heart turns soft and vibrant.

I'm grateful for nature's gifts and the coexistence of human civilization,
Enriching and bringing joy to my perception of the world.

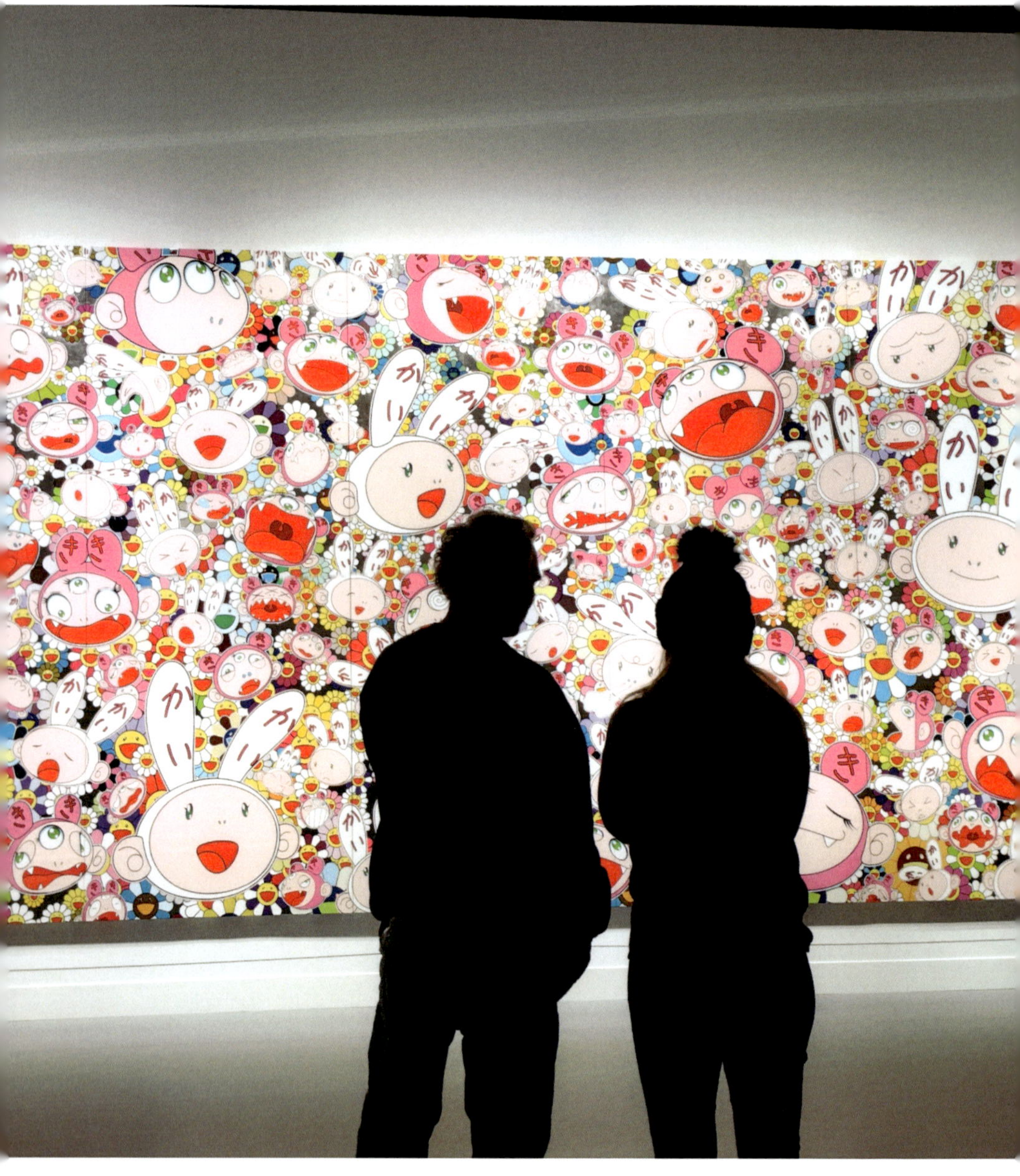

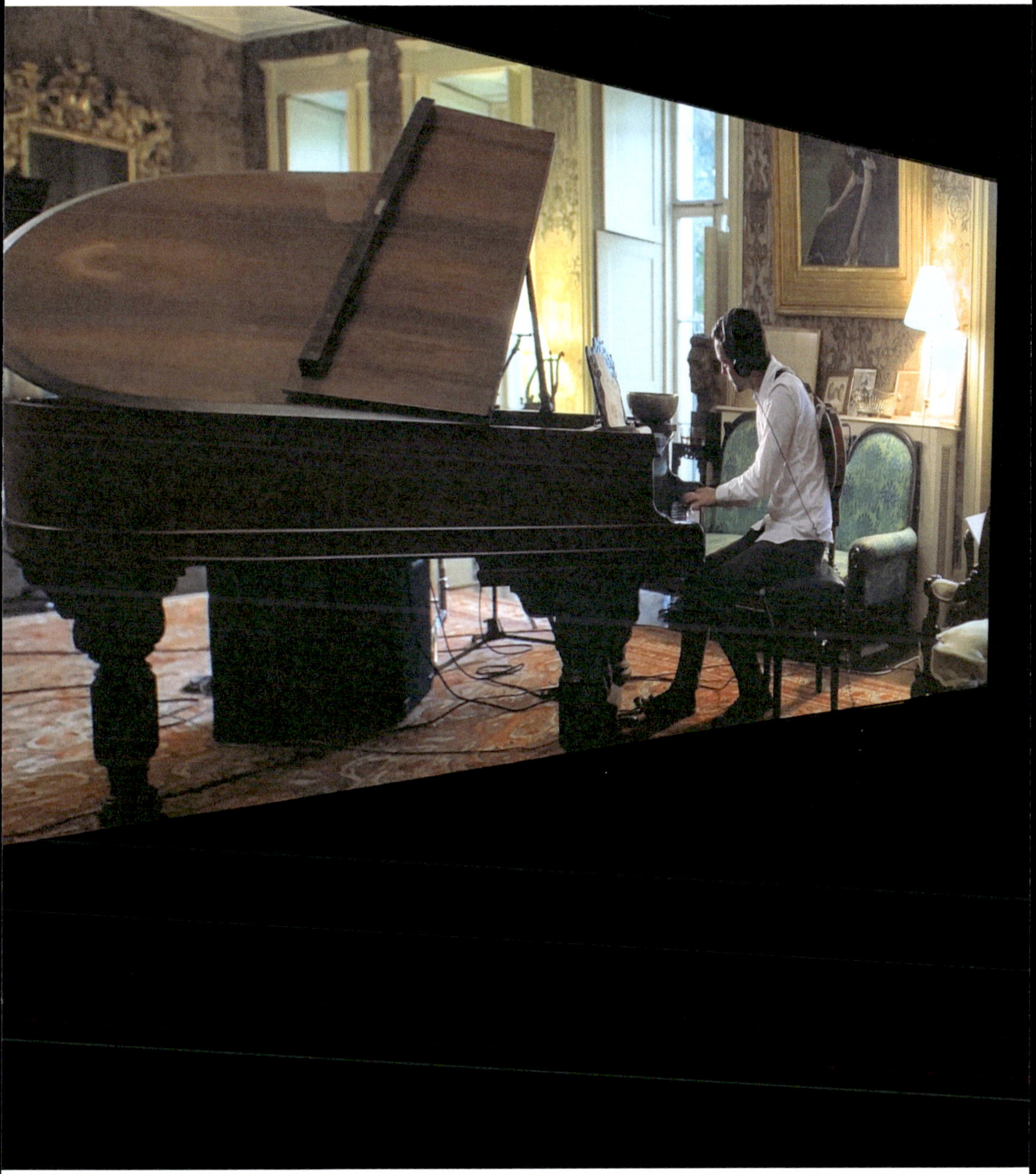

21

二十一岁
我害怕走得太慢
会被同行的队友们落下
又担心因为走得过于匆忙
会在到达终点线时
遗憾地错过沿途的美丽风景

于是我一路上都内心忐忑
惴惴不安
不经意间
青春过半

Twenty-one

At twenty-one,
I fear progressing too slowly,
Afraid of being left behind by my peers.
Yet, I worry that rushing too hastily
Will make me regretfully miss the beauty along the way.

So, throughout the journey,
I am uneasy,
Anxious,
And, without realizing,
Half of my youth has passed.

朋友？笔友？

Charlotte的爱犬Sky一月份平静地去世了
她说她去了动物庇护所重新领养了一只
取名Darty
她今年去了意大利罗马旅行
现在依然住在自己海边的房子
喜欢现在的生活和状态

她说最近翻旧物
看到离开中国前
我送她的一张明信片
她说今天收到我的邮件的一瞬间
就不自主地笑了起来

翻看邮件收件箱
我和Ben上次联络
已经是2018年的时候的事了
从中国回到英国后
他攻读了牛津大学的博士
随后辗转于英国和德国的大学
做项目研究和交流
他跟我分享了一些在德国生活的照片
说一直保存着我去厦门鼓浪屿时
邮寄给他的那张明信片
他现在回到英国
继续在一所大学教书和做研究

我和Charlotte还有Ben
十年前在中国国内相识
后来他们结束了在中国的工作和旅行
回到了英国
这些年我们便以邮件的方式
断断续续地交流往来

他们总是谦虚低调 彬彬有礼
所以我们的谈话无论是面对面
还是邮件里
都让人觉得很舒服也很享受

我们之间的友情蛮奇妙
第一次和Charlotte相识的时候
她一口优雅的伦敦腔
言谈得体 带着一种特别的温度
那种感觉
瞬间把那个热爱欧洲文化的我
带到了英国

她讲话节奏不紧不慢
待人自然真诚
跟她的交流总是让我觉得放松

刚认识Ben时
第一印象他有几分书呆子气
话少但做事认真严谨

我第一次爬华山的经历
是他当时和去西安旅行的朋友Rachel一起的
到现在依然是我最美好的经历之一
后来见他写汉字时
真的是自愧不如
他字迹工整 干净有力
加上那股认真劲
所以他后来作为英国学者访问德国
我一点也不意外
由于他太过接地气也很认真生活
我常常忽略和忘记
他是一个有着国际视角且热爱科学的学者

人跟人的缘分很奇妙
没想到当时在国内相识的朋友
如今成为了跨越半个地球的笔友
距离上我们变得遥远
内心我们却依然参与到才彼此的生活里
这就是所谓的
海内存知己 天涯若比邻吧

7
Memo-writing

Friends? Pen-pals?

Charlotte's beloved dog Sky peacefully passed away in January.
She mentioned adopting a new one from an animal shelter, named Darty.
This year, she traveled to Rome, Italy.
Currently residing in her seaside house,
She enjoys her present life and state of being.

She mentioned going through old things recently
And came across a postcard I sent her before leaving China.
She said she couldn't help but smile the moment she received my email today.

Checking my email inbox,
The last contact I had with Ben was back in 2018.
After returning from China to the UK,
He pursued a Ph.D. at a university in Oxford,
Later moving between universities in the UK and Germany for project research and exchanges.
He shared some photos of his life in Germany,
Mentioning he still keeps the postcard I sent him when I visited Gulangyu in Xiamen, China.
He's back in the UK now,
Continuing to teach and conduct research at a university.

Charlotte, Ben, and I
Met each other in China ten years ago.
After concluding their work and travels in China,
They returned to the UK,
And over the years, we've been intermittently communicating via email.

They've always been modest and polite,
So whether our conversations are face-to-face
Or within emails,
I always sense a feeling of comfortableness and enjoy the interaction.

The friendship between us is quite peculiar.
The first time I met Charlotte,
Her elegant London accent,
Polite and warm demeanor,
Instantly transported me who loved European culture to the UK.

Her speech is unhurried,
Her interactions are natural and sincere,
Talking to her always makes me feel relaxed.

When I first met Ben,
He gave off a somewhat nerdy vibe,
Reserved in speech but serious and meticulous in action.
My first experience climbing Mount Hua
Was with him and his friend Rachel during a trip to Xi'an.
It remains one of my most cherished experiences to this day.
Later, seeing him write Chinese characters,
I truly felt inferior.
His handwriting is neat, clean, and powerful,
Coupled with his seriousness,
So I wasn't surprised when he later visited Germany as a British scholar.
Because of his down-to-earth and serious approach to life,
I often overlook and forget
That he is a scholar with an international perspective and a love for science.

The connections between people are interesting.
Friends I met back in China
Now become pen pals spanning half the globe.
Though distance between us remains long,
In our hearts, we remain a part of each other's lives.
This is what they call
"Confidants in the sea are like neighbors even as far as the end of the world."

Brown University, United States

我

生命里的每一个人
都像是一片拼图
他们拼在一起组成了完整的我

任何一个人的到来
我的世界便多了一种色彩
任何一个人的离开
我的世界就缺少了一块

Me

Every person in my life
Is a piece of a puzzle
They fit together forming the complete me

With each person's arrival
My world gains a new hue
With each person's departure
My world becomes incomplete

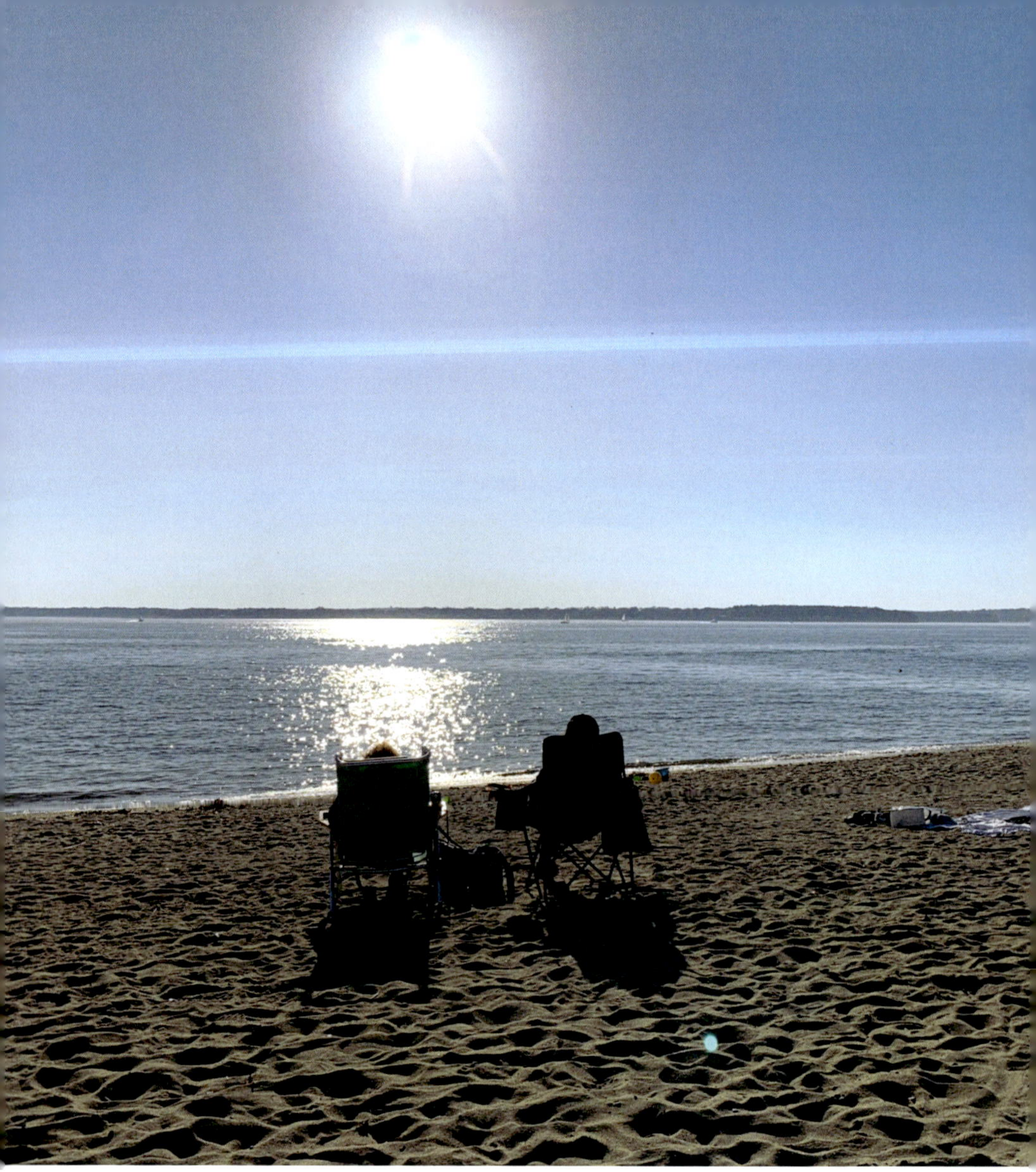

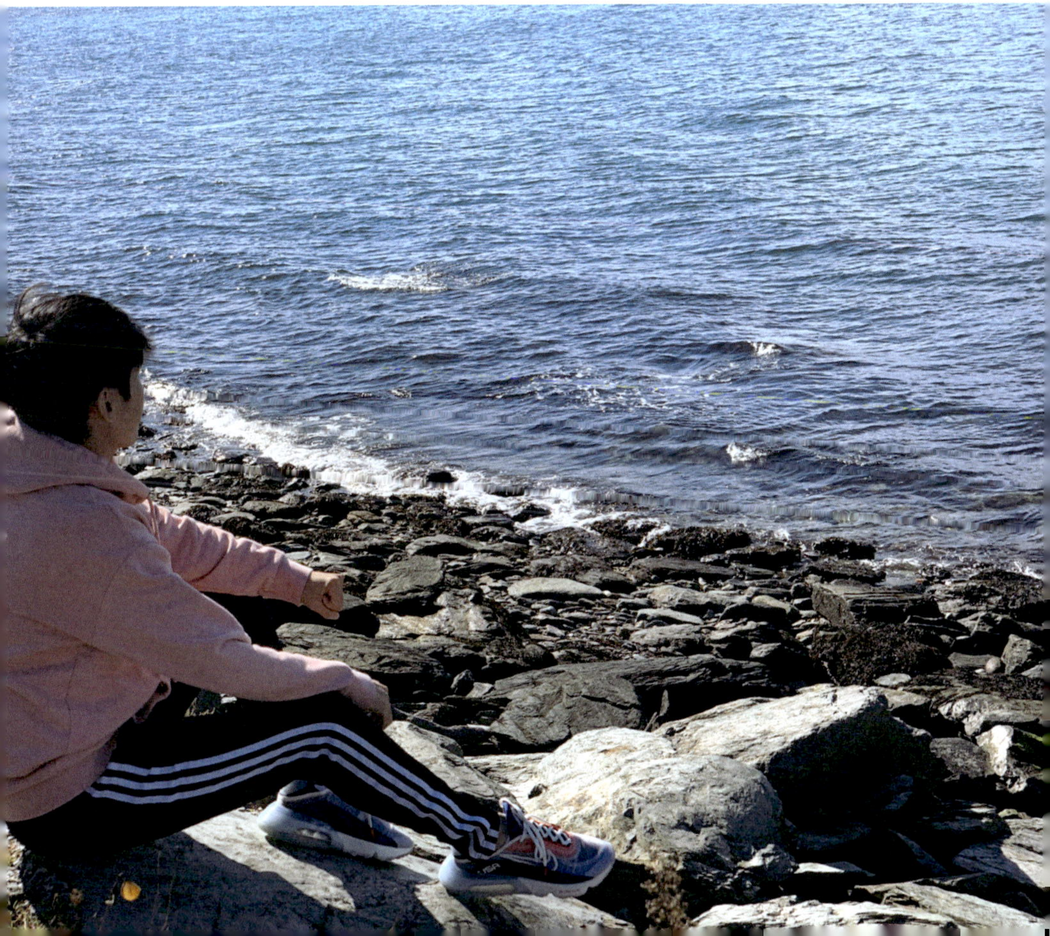

自由

自由
就是与自然在一起

自由
就是身体允许我去到自己想去的地方

自由
就是打开自己

自由
和孤独很多时候是在一起的
是我建立的宇宙

Free

Freedom is being with nature.

Freedom is when my body allowing me to go wherever you want.

Freedom is opening myself up.

Freedom and loneliness are often together,
They form the universe i create.

自由

不被外界声音干扰
不因为别人的标准和成就自我评判

正视和接纳自己的不足
专注在自己的跑道
自己的追求和梦想
自己的优点和长处
自己每天生活点滴

这本身就是自由

Free

Not disturbed by external voices,
Not self-judging based on other people's standards and achievements,
Facing and accepting my own shortcomings,
Focusing on my own path,
Pursuits and dreams,
Strengths and virtues,
Moments of my daily life,

This, in itself, is freedom to me.

爱·自由

让你想走就走的旅行 是去哪里
让你想见就能立刻就去见的人 是谁
让你不用特别考虑代价 很热爱的事 是什么
让你一想起来就兴奋激动 眼里发光的事 是什么

Love · Free

A journey that beckons you to explore, where does it lead?
A person you can meet immediately between a thought, who could that be?
A passion so profound, where the joy outweighs the need to think about the cost, what is it?
An endeavor that fills you with excitement the moment you rise, making your eyes sparkle with anticipation, what could it be?

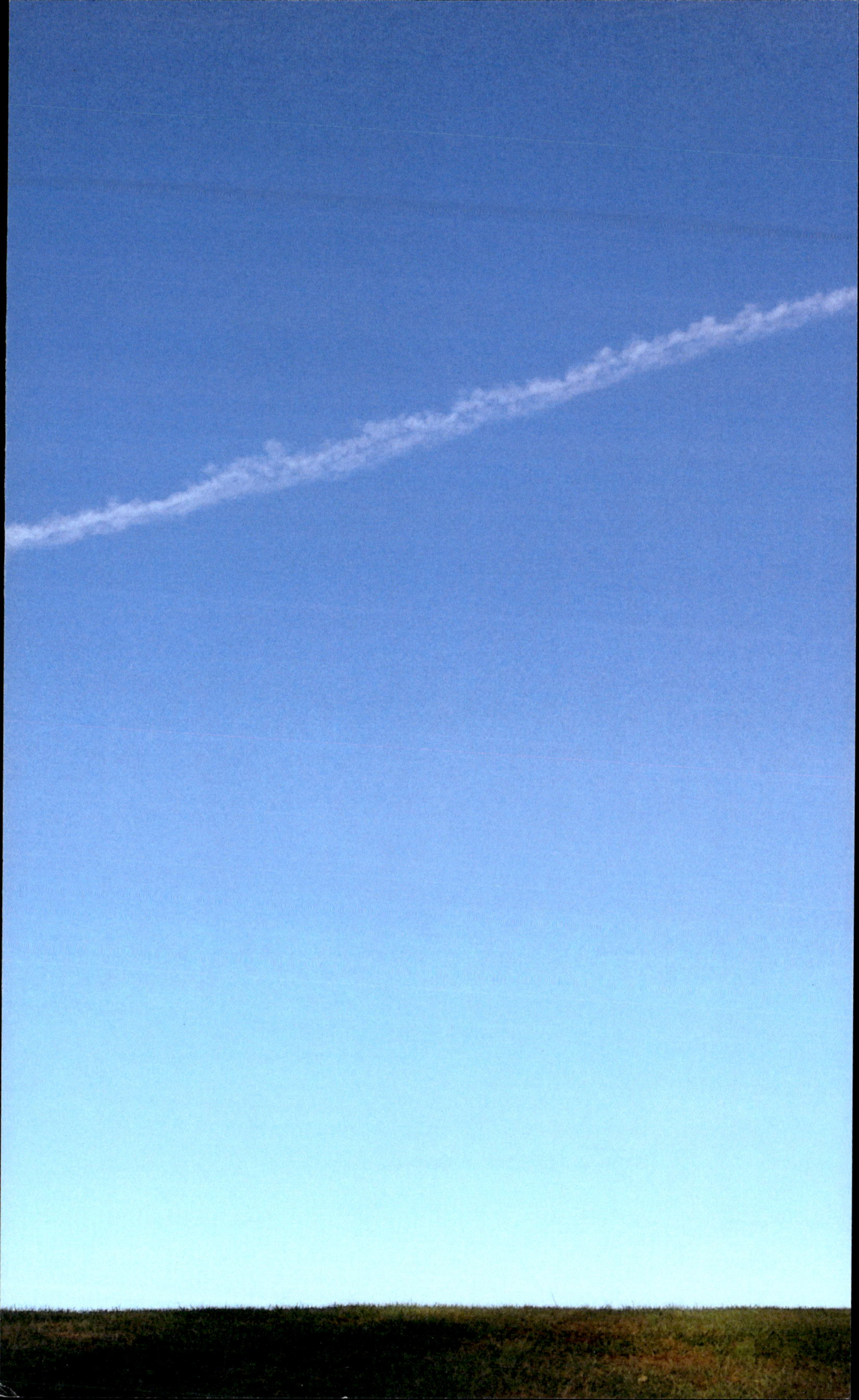

愿你对这个世界好奇
愿你真诚热烈
愿你依旧少年

May you be curious about this world,
May you be sincere and passionate,
May you remain forever young.

About the Author

Bo Zhang (张博) is an educator, researcher, and writer holding a doctoral degree in Educational Leadership from the University of Hartford in the United States. Originally from China, Bo now resides in Rhode Island, U.S. During spare time, Bo enjoys writing, traveling, photography, and filmmaking.

Books also from Bo:

1. 22023: 迟开的花 A Poetry Memoir
2. Crossing Borders, Bridging Cultures: The Narratives of Global Scholars
3. Structural Wonders: Diverse Architecture in the United States
4. The Ocean State: Rhode Island
5. Lost in Blue
6. Snapshots of a Stranger in a Strange Land: An International Student in the United States

The Cliff Walk
Rhode Island, United States

The University of Massachusetts Boston
United States

Milton Keynes UK
Ingram Content Group UK Ltd.
UKRC041144070124
435573UK00006B/51